The Ultimate Cuisinart Bread Machine Cookbook

96 Foolproof Bread Machine Recipes for White, Whole Wheat, Sweet, and Gluten-Free Loaves — Easy Step-by-Step Guide to Perfect Homemade Bread Every Time"

Abigail Douglas

Table of Contents

The Ultimate Cuisinart Bread Machine Cookbook 1

Preface 23

Introduction 27

    Welcome to Your Cuisinart Bakery 27

    Why Homemade Bread Beats Store-Bought Every Time 28

    Bread-Making Basics: What You Actually Need to Know 29

    Reader Promise: What You Can Expect from This Book 30

Chapter 1 34

Understanding Your Machine 34

Cuisinart Models & Settings: What You're Working With 35

    Common Features Across Models: 35

Parts of the Machine: Know Each Component 37

Programs & Cycles: What Each Setting Does 38

When to Press What (And When Not To) 41

Let Your Machine Work for You 42

Chapter 2 44

    Bread-Making Essentials 44

    Ingredient Roles Explained 45

        Flour – The Foundation 45

Water (or Milk) – The Moisture 46

Yeast – The Lift 47

Sugar (or Honey) – The Fuel and the Flavor 47

Salt – The Silent Hero 48

Fat – The Softener 49

Extras – Seeds, Nuts, Fruits, Herbs 49

Proper Measuring Tips 49

Measuring Flour the Right Way 50

Measuring Liquids Accurately 50

Measuring Yeast, Salt, Sugar, etc. 51

Order of Ingredients: Why It Matters 51

Pantry-Friendly Options & Ingredient Swaps 52

Chapter 3 56

Troubleshooting Your Loaf 56

Common Mistakes Solved 57

Loaf Is Too Dense or Heavy 57

Loaf Rose, Then Collapsed 58

Gummy or Undercooked Center 59

Crust Too Thick or Hard 60

Ingredients Didn't Mix Properly 61

Fixes & Preventative Tips 62

Chapter 4 67

White Breads – Soft, Fluffy, Versatile 67

How These Recipes Work 67

1. Classic White Sandwich Bread 68

2. Farmhouse Buttermilk Loaf 69

3. Country White Honey Bread 70

4. Crusty French White Bread 70

5. Milk & Butter White Bread 71

6. Olive Oil Country Loaf 72

7. Garlic Herb White Bread 72

8. Mozzarella Basil White Bread 73

9. Onion Dill Bread 74

10. Sesame White Loaf 75

11. Parmesan Herb Bread 75

12. Yogurt & Honey White Bread 76

13. Potato White Bread 77

14. Southern Cornmeal White Bread 78

15. White Dinner Rolls (Pan Baked) 78

16. Cheddar White Bread 79

17. Greek Yogurt White Bread 80

18. Rustic Italian Loaf 81

19. Soft Pull-Apart Bread (Use Dough Cycle) 81

20. Beginner's Everyday White Bread 82

Chapter 5 85

Whole Wheat & Multigrain Breads – Nutritious and Fiber-Rich 85

Recipe Notes 86

1. 100% Whole Wheat Sandwich Bread 86

2. Honey Wheat Bread 87

3. Oatmeal Wheat Loaf 87

4. Flaxseed & Wheat Fiber Bread 87

5. Multigrain Seed Bread 88

6. Cinnamon Raisin Wheat Bread 88

7. Sunflower Seed Whole Wheat 88

8. Molasses Wheat Loaf 89

9. Cracked Wheat Rustic Bread 89

10. Barley & Wheat Country Bread 89

11. Rye-Infused Wheat Bread 90

12. Chia & Quinoa Wheat Loaf 90

13. Whole Wheat English Muffin Bread 90

14. Harvest Grain Bread 91

15. Spelt & Wheat Loaf 91

16. Millet Multigrain Bread 91

17. Ancient Grains Power Bread 92

18. Apple Walnut Wheat Bread 92

19. Brown Rice & Wheat Bread 92

20. Hearty Breakfast Wheat Loaf 93

Chapter 6 95

Sweet Breads & Treat Loaves – Perfect for Breakfast or Dessert 95

1. Classic Cinnamon Swirl Bread 96

2. Chocolate Chip Brioche 96

3. Banana Nut Bread 96

4. Apple Cinnamon Bread 97

5. Sweet Vanilla Milk Bread 97

6. Pumpkin Spice Loaf 97

7. Blueberry Lemon Bread 98

8. Maple Pecan Breakfast Bread 98

9. Almond Coconut Bread 98

10. Raisin Date Loaf 99

11. Honey Butter Bread 99

12. Mocha Chocolate Bread 99

13. Strawberry Cream Cheese Bread 99

14. Carrot Cake Bread.. 100

15. Pineapple Coconut Bread.................................. 100

16. Gingerbread Loaf... 101

17. Cherry Almond Sweet Bread 101

18. Orange Cranberry Loaf................................... 101

19. Marshmallow Chocolate Swirl Bread............ 101

20. Birthday Cake Bread....................................... 102

Chapter 7 104

Gluten-Free Breads – Soft, Satisfying, and Wheat-Free

.... 104

Tips for Gluten-Free Bread Success 105

15 Gluten-Free Bread Machine Recipes................. 105

1. Classic Gluten-Free White Bread 105

2. Gluten-Free Multigrain Sandwich Bread 106

3. Brown Rice & Quinoa Bread 106

4. Oat Flour Bread (GF Certified Oats) 106

5. Almond Flour Banana Bread 107

6. Gluten-Free Cinnamon Raisin Bread 107

7. Soft Gluten-Free Dinner Rolls (use dough cycle) 108

8. Buckwheat Honey Bread 108

9. Gluten-Free Pumpkin Bread 108

10. Coconut Flour Sweet Bread 109

11. Gluten-Free Sourdough-Style Bread 109

12. Cheesy Herb Gluten-Free Bread 109

13. Golden Cornbread Loaf (GF) 110

14. Flax & Chia Gluten-Free Bread 110

15. High-Protein Gluten-Free Power Bread 110

Chapter 8 112

International & Specialty Breads – Flavors of the World from Your Countertop 112

11 Global & Specialty Bread Machine Recipes 113

1. Japanese Milk Bread (Shokupan) 113

2. Irish Soda Bread (Machine-Adapted) 113

3. German Potato Bread 114

4. Cuban Bread (Pan Cubano) 114

5. Moroccan Olive Bread (Khobz Zaitoun) 114

6. Swedish Cardamom Bread (Kardemummabröd) 115

7. Indian Spiced Bread 115

8. Turkish Pide Bread (Machine-Mixed) 116

9. Scandinavian Rye Bread 116

10. Caribbean Coconut Bread 116

11. Mediterranean Herb Focaccia (Machine-Mixed) 117

Chapter 9 119

Seasonal & Holiday Loaves – Festive Bakes That Make Memories 119

5 Seasonal & Holiday Bread Machine Recipes 120

   1. Classic Challah (Dough Cycle) 120

   2. Pumpkin Spice Harvest Loaf 120

   3. Italian Panettone-Style Bread 121

   4. Cinnamon Cranberry Christmas Bread 121

   5. Easter Lemon Poppy Seed Loaf 121

Chapter 10 123

Beyond the Loaf – Doughs & Rolls (5 Recipes) 123

5 Dough & Roll Recipes for Your Bread Machine .. 124

   1. Classic Dinner Rolls 124

   2. Garlic Herb Knots 124

   3. New York–Style Pizza Dough 124

4. Soft Pretzels 125

5. Cinnamon Swirl Rolls 125

Chapter 11 127

7-Day Beginner Bread Bootcamp 127

The 7-Day Plan 127

Day 1 – Simple White Sandwich Bread 127

Day 2 – Honey Wheat Bread 128

Day 3 – Cinnamon Raisin Breakfast Bread 128

Day 4 – Rustic French Loaf 128

Day 5 – Multigrain Energy Bread 129

Day 6 – Gluten-Free Sandwich Bread 129

Day 7 – Celebration Sweet Bread 129

Chapter 12 133

Storing, Slicing & Serving Your Bread 133

Best Storage Techniques 133

Proper Slicing Tools 134

Serving Suggestions 134

Chapter 13 137

Make It Your Way – Customizing Recipes 137

Add-Ins & Flavors 137

Dietary Modifications 138

Boosting Nutrition 139

Chapter 14 141

Ingredient Conversion Guide 141

Chapter 15 146

Bread Machine Glossary 146

Acknowledgments 150

Copyright © 2025 by Abigail Douglas

All rights reserved. No part of this book may be copied, reproduced, stored, or transmitted in any form or by any means—electronic, mechanical, photocopying, recording, or otherwise without prior written permission from the publisher, except for brief quotations used in reviews or scholarly works.

Disclaimer

The information, recipes, and suggestions provided in The Effortless Bread Machine Cookbook are intended for general informational and educational purposes only. While every effort has been made to ensure accuracy and clarity, the author and publisher make no guarantees regarding results, as outcomes may vary based on the brand and model of bread machine used, ingredient quality, altitude, climate, and individual kitchen practices.

This cookbook is not a substitute for professional dietary advice, medical guidance, or allergen management. If you have food allergies, dietary restrictions, or health conditions, please consult with a qualified healthcare provider or nutritionist before trying any new recipe.

All recipes are developed with standard home kitchen equipment and widely available ingredients. Always read and follow the safety instructions provided by your bread machine manufacturer before operating your appliance.

The author and publisher disclaim any liability, loss, or risk incurred as a consequence—direct or indirect—of the use and application of any of the content in this book.

All product names, brands, or references to appliances are used for descriptive purposes only and are not affiliated with or endorsed by this publication.

22

Preface

There's something magical about bread baking—how a handful of simple ingredients can fill your kitchen with warmth, comfort, and the irresistible scent of home. For centuries, bread has been more than just food; it's been a symbol of togetherness, tradition, and nourishment. Today, with modern kitchen appliances like the Cuisinart bread machine, you can bring that same magic into your home effortlessly—no matter your skill level.

When I first began experimenting with bread machines, I was amazed at how quickly I could produce bakery-quality loaves without kneading for hours or fussing over rising times. Whether it was a soft white sandwich bread for my family's lunches, a hearty whole wheat loaf packed with fiber, a decadent cinnamon swirl breakfast bread, or a tender gluten-free creation for friends with dietary needs, my Cuisinart bread maker became my most trusted kitchen companion.

This cookbook was born out of a desire to share that experience with you—not just through recipes, but through clear guidance, troubleshooting tips, and creative variations that will make your bread-making journey foolproof and fun. Inside, you'll find 101 easy bread machine recipes covering classic white breads, nutritious whole grain loaves, sweet breads and dessert-style treats, gluten-free breads, and international favorites. Each recipe has been tested for reliability, flavor, and texture, ensuring you'll achieve perfect results every time.

Beyond recipes, this book gives you a deep understanding of how your Cuisinart bread maker works—machine settings, bread cycles, ingredient roles, and storage tips—so you can adapt, customize, and create your own signature loaves with confidence. I've also included a 7-Day Beginner Bread Bootcamp for those who want to build their skills one loaf at a time.

Whether you're baking your first loaf or upgrading your bread-making skills, this guide is your ticket to bread that's fresher, healthier, and more satisfying than anything store-bought. With the help of your Cuisinart bread machine, you'll unlock a world of possibilities:

- Homemade sandwich bread that stays soft for days
- Whole wheat and multigrain breads packed with flavor and nutrition
- Sweet, aromatic loaves perfect for breakfast or dessert
- Gluten-free breads with tender crumb and no compromise on taste
- Artisan and international breads to expand your kitchen repertoire

From my kitchen to yours, I invite you to roll up your sleeves, press that start button, and let the irresistible smell of freshly baked bread transform your home. Your new bread-baking adventure starts here.

Introduction

Welcome to Your Cuisinart Bakery

There's something deeply grounding—almost spiritual about the scent of freshly baked bread drifting through a kitchen. It evokes memories. It slows us down. It reminds us we're home.

Now, with your Cuisinart bread machine, that feeling doesn't have to wait for a trip to the farmers' market or a rare weekend off. It's yours any day, any time, at the push of a button.

This book was born from a love of that feeling and a desire to make it available to everyone, no matter your schedule, baking experience, or dietary needs. Whether you're here to master classic white sandwich bread, explore gluten-free loaves, or bring international favorites to your family table, welcome. You're in the right kitchen.

This isn't just a cookbook. It's your new bread companion. It's here to guide, support, and inspire you from your very first loaf to your fiftieth.

Why Homemade Bread Beats Store-Bought Every Time

Let's be honest—store-bought bread just doesn't compare. The ingredients list alone is enough to raise eyebrows: preservatives, conditioners, artificial flavors, and sugar overloads in loaves that were designed for shelf life, not soul.

When you bake your own bread at home, especially with a machine as intuitive as the Cuisinart, something changes. You take control of every ingredient. You eliminate the guesswork. You feed your family real food, made with real love. And perhaps best of all, it's not complicated.

Your machine does the mixing, kneading, rising, and

baking. You just choose your ingredients, press a few buttons, and let the magic unfold.

And the payoff? That moment when the machine beeps, the lid opens, and the scent of warm, golden crust fills the room. That's your reward.

Bread-Making Basics: What You Actually Need to Know

If you've never made bread before, let me tell you: you do not need a chef's degree, or even a rolling pin.

Bread making in a Cuisinart is simple—but like any art, there are a few things to understand upfront:

- **Flour matters.** Bread flour yields better structure than all-purpose. But don't worry—we'll walk you through when and how to use each type.

- **Yeast is alive.** It needs warmth, sugar, and time. Treat it right, and it'll reward you with lift and airiness.

- **Order is everything.** In most recipes, liquids go in first, then dry ingredients, and yeast last. This keeps the machine happy and the rise reliable.

- **Precision wins.** Measuring ingredients accurately (especially flour) is one of the most important skills to develop. But don't worry—we'll show you how to do it right.

Each recipe in this book is written with simplicity in mind. You'll also find customization tips if you're dairy-free, gluten-free, or experimenting with flavors.

Your job? Trust the process. You're going to make beautiful bread.

Reader Promise: What You Can Expect from This

Book

This cookbook was created for everyday people—home cooks, parents, empty-nesters, beginners, curious bakers, and everyone in between. If you've got a loaf pan in your heart and a Cuisinart on your counter, this book is your new best friend.

Inside, you'll find:

- **101 foolproof recipes**, divided clearly by type: white, whole wheat, sweet, gluten-free, and more.
- **Minimal prep time** and **easy-to-follow instructions** with ingredients you can pronounce.
- **Tips for troubleshooting**, storing, slicing, and reinventing your bread.
- **Inspiration**—so you don't just bake, but enjoy the process.

Whether you're baking for Sunday brunch, a school lunchbox, a gluten-sensitive friend, or just yourself on a rainy afternoon, know this: You are fully capable of making bread that impresses.

So take a deep breath. Preheat your excitement. And let's bake something unforgettable.

PART 1: MASTERING YOUR CUISINART BREAD MACHINE

Chapter 1

Understanding Your Machine

Your Bread Companion, Unplugged and Understood

Every masterpiece begins with understanding the tools you're using—and with bread, your Cuisinart bread machine is the artist's easel, oven, timer, and hands. It's more than a gadget. It's a trustworthy kitchen companion built to take the guesswork out of bread-making and deliver consistent results loaf after loaf.

Whether you own the **CBK-110**, **CBK-200**, or another model in the Cuisinart family, they all share one common promise: *homemade bread, made simple.*

But before we dive into our first dough, let's take a few minutes to explore what your machine actually does and how to work with it, not against it.

Cuisinart Models & Settings: What You're Working With

Your specific Cuisinart model might have unique features, but most share a similar control layout, menu system, and functionality. Here's a general look at what you can expect:

Common Features Across Models:

- **Pre-Programmed Menu Cycles** (usually 12–16): Each one is designed for different types of bread or dough.
- **Loaf Size Options**: Typically 1 lb, 1.5 lb, and 2 lb.
- **Crust Color Control**: Light, Medium, Dark.
- **Delay Timer**: Allows you to set the machine up to 13 hours ahead—wake up to fresh bread.

- **Keep Warm Function**: Keeps your loaf warm after baking for up to 60 minutes.

If You're Using the CBK-200 or CBK-110:

- CBK-200 includes a **convection fan**, which helps bake crisper crusts and even textures.
- CBK-110 is compact, with a user-friendly LCD display and a more basic design—great for beginners.
- Both machines include a **gluten-free setting**, a **rapid bake function**, and audible tones for add-ins (nuts, fruits).

Pro Tip: Look in your machine's manual for a list of menu cycles. We'll refer to the program number (e.g., Menu 1, Menu 9) in this book to help you match the recipe to the correct setting.

Parts of the Machine: Know Each Component

Let's lift the lid—literally—and get familiar with what's inside:

1. Lid & Viewing Window

You'll likely peek through this window more times than you expect. It lets you watch the mixing and rising process without lifting the lid (which can cause heat loss or deflation).

2. Control Panel & LCD Screen

This is your command center. Use the menu button to scroll through programs, select loaf size, and choose crust shade. The start/pause and stop buttons control the action.

3. Baking Pan (Removable)

This nonstick pan is where the magic happens. All ingredients go into the pan in a specific order. It locks into place at the bottom of the machine.

4. Kneading Paddle

Attached inside the pan, this does the heavy work: mixing, kneading, and folding the dough. Most recipes use one paddle—some models come with a spare or twin paddles.

5. Heating Element

Hidden in the base of the machine, it provides even, direct heat during the bake cycle.

Programs & Cycles: What Each Setting Does

Most Cuisinart bread makers offer between 12–16 automatic programs. Here's a simplified breakdown of what you'll typically find, though the names may vary slightly:

Cycle	Purpose
1. Basic/White	For standard white and light wheat bread recipes

2. French	Longer rise, chewier crust, airy interior—ideal for artisan-style loaves
3. Whole Wheat	For denser breads made with whole grain flours
4. Sweet	Designed for sugar-rich or fruit-laced breads
5. Gluten-Free	Custom cycle for gluten-free dough to improve texture
6. ExpressBake/Rapid	Cuts baking time significantly; great when you need bread fast
7. Dough Only	Mixes and kneads dough but doesn't bake—useful

	for pizza, rolls, pretzels
8. Pasta Dough	For mixing and kneading pasta dough
9. Jam	Yes, some models make jam or preserves directly in the bread machine
10. Bake Only	No mixing, just baking—perfect for re-baking underdone loaves
11. Artisan/Crusty	For extra crusty or bakery-style loaves with longer fermentation
12. Custom/Manual	Lets you adjust rise/knead/bake times manually (advanced use)

Note: Check your user manual for the exact order of your machine's cycles—this cookbook will help match your recipe with the correct one.

When to Press What (And When Not To)

Don't worry—you won't need to memorize everything. But here are a few golden rules for working with your machine:

- **Don't open the lid during kneading**—unless you're scraping down flour or checking texture (early in the cycle).
- **Avoid opening during rising or baking**. Heat loss can collapse your loaf.
- **Wait before removing the pan after baking**. The loaf firms up as it cools slightly—removing it too fast can tear the bottom crust.

- **Use oven mitts.** That pan gets hot.

Let Your Machine Work for You

The true beauty of the Cuisinart bread machine lies in what it frees you from: kneading by hand, babysitting dough, second-guessing the bake. This chapter was just your introduction. The rest of this book is your roadmap to becoming the kind of home baker who always has something golden on the cooling rack—and maybe a few neighbors knocking at the door.

You're ready. Let's make bread.

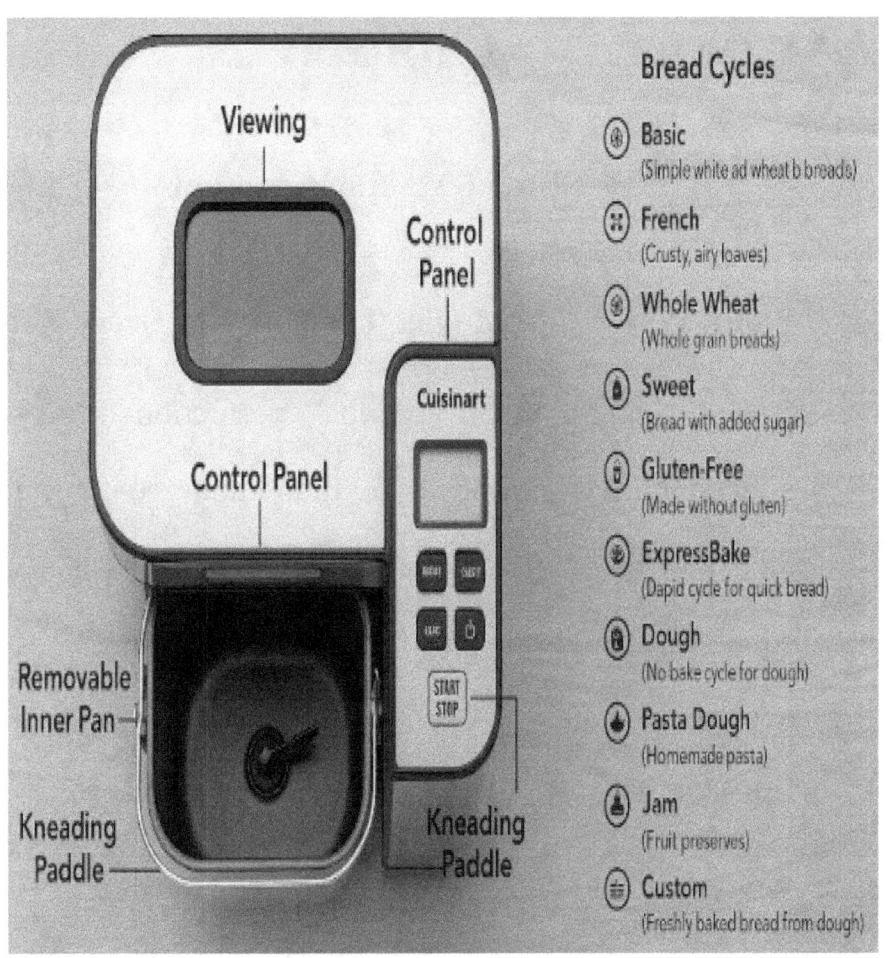

Chapter 2

Bread-Making Essentials

Flour, Water, and Magic: The Heart of Every Loaf

Baking bread isn't about perfection—it's about understanding. And once you grasp the essential building blocks of bread, you'll start to see every loaf as a simple equation you can trust. This chapter isn't here to overwhelm you with chemistry. It's here to give you quiet confidence before you press start.

We're going to break down:

- What each ingredient does (and how to treat it)
- How to measure properly (so your machine doesn't struggle)
- The correct order of ingredients (this matters more than you think)
- Smart swaps and pantry-friendly substitutions

Whether you're baking a white sandwich loaf or a gluten-free oat bread, the same principles apply.

Ingredient Roles Explained

Each ingredient in your bread has a job—and skipping, substituting, or mis-measuring even one can change the texture, rise, or taste.

Let's get to know your new best friends:

Flour – The Foundation

Flour gives your bread its structure. The most common types you'll use in this book are:

- **Bread flour** – High in protein (gluten), gives structure and chew. Best for most recipes.
- **All-purpose flour** – Works in a pinch, but may lead to slightly softer structure.

- **Whole wheat flour** – Dense, nutritious, and hearty. Usually combined with bread flour.
- **Gluten-free flour blends** – Pre-mixed to mimic gluten. Not interchangeable with wheat flour.

Water (or Milk) – The Moisture

Liquid activates the yeast, binds the dough, and affects texture.

- **Water** is neutral, light, and common in most recipes.
- **Milk** adds softness and a slight sweetness—great for white, enriched, or sweet breads.
- **Too much liquid?** Bread collapses.
- **Too little?** It won't rise properly.

Yeast – The Lift

Yeast is the soul of the bread. It feeds on sugar, creates carbon dioxide, and causes the dough to rise.

Types you'll see in this book:

- **Instant yeast** (also called rapid-rise): No proofing needed. Just add to dry ingredients.
- **Active dry yeast:** Slightly slower rise. Can be swapped 1:1 with instant, but may benefit from a warm-water proof.

Do not use fresh or cake yeast *in your bread machine—it's not designed for it.*

Sugar (or Honey) – The Fuel and the Flavor

Sugar feeds the yeast and also adds color and flavor to

your crust. In sweet loaves, it's essential. In savory breads, it's usually just a tablespoon.

- You can substitute honey or maple syrup 1:1 (reduce liquids slightly).
- Avoid artificial sweeteners unless the recipe specifies—they don't feed yeast.

Salt – The Silent Hero

Salt strengthens gluten, controls the yeast's rise, and adds flavor.

Too much salt = slow rise or no rise.

Too little = flat flavor and overexpansion.

Never place salt directly on top of yeast in the machine—it can deactivate it. Always keep them separate in the pan.

Fat – The Softener

Fats like butter, oil, or eggs make bread tender and richer.

- **Butter** = flavor, color, softness
- **Oil** = softness, longer shelf life
- **Eggs** = structure + richness (used in brioche, sweet breads)

Extras – Seeds, Nuts, Fruits, Herbs

These make bread magical but timing matters.

Let your machine alert you when it's time to add mix-ins (you'll hear a beep). Add-ins too early can break down during kneading and affect structure.

Proper Measuring Tips

In bread making, precision is everything.

A little too much flour can turn a beautiful loaf into a brick. A little too much water can collapse the top like a deflated balloon. But don't panic—it's easy to get right once you know how.

Measuring Flour the Right Way

Scoop and level. Don't pack.

1. Use a spoon to scoop flour into your measuring cup.
2. Level it off with a flat edge (like a knife).
3. Don't shake the cup or press it down.

This avoids overpacking, which can add up to 25% too much flour.

Measuring Liquids Accurately

Use a clear liquid measuring cup.

- Place on a flat surface and check at eye level.
- Always measure cold liquids cold and warm liquids warm.

Measuring Yeast, Salt, Sugar, etc.

Use dry measuring spoons for accuracy.

- Fill the spoon and level off with a knife or straight edge.
- Don't use heaping spoonfuls.

Order of Ingredients: Why It Matters

Your Cuisinart bread machine mixes from the bottom up, and how ingredients interact before mixing can affect the rise and texture.

Always follow this order unless your machine says otherwise:

1. **Liquids** (water, milk, oil, eggs)
2. **Sweeteners** (sugar, honey)
3. **Salt**
4. **Flour** (create a mound on top)
5. **Yeast** (placed last, on top of the flour—not touching liquids)

Why?

If yeast gets wet too soon (especially with salt), it activates too early—or dies. This weakens your rise.

In some rapid cycles or gluten-free recipes, you may mix dry ingredients first or use slightly different layering. We'll walk you through those exceptions in each recipe.

Pantry-Friendly Options & Ingredient Swaps

Real bread isn't about fancy ingredients. It's about flexibility.

Here are a few swap-friendly, budget-conscious options to keep on hand:

If You're Out of...	Try This Instead
Milk	Water + 1 tbsp butter or milk powder
Bread Flour	All-purpose flour + 1 tsp vital wheat gluten per cup
Butter	Neutral oil (like canola or olive)
Honey	Maple syrup, agave, or brown sugar
Eggs (for richness)	1 tbsp Greek yogurt or 1 tbsp nut butter

Nuts/Dried Fruit	Chocolate chips, seeds, citrus zest, or herbs

Gluten-free readers: Make sure swaps are certified GF. Don't mix regular flour into a gluten-free recipe—it changes everything.

You're Almost Ready to Bake

By understanding how ingredients work and how to treat them right—you've already leveled up. Now, every time you measure flour, pour water, or sprinkle yeast, you'll know why you're doing it. That's the difference between following a recipe and becoming a real home baker.

In the next chapters, we'll explore exactly what to bake, with foolproof recipes written just for your Cuisinart. All you need is a few ingredients, a little curiosity, and a hungry kitchen.

Are you ready to start baking?

Chapter 3

Troubleshooting Your Loaf

It's Not You—It's the Loaf (and We'll Fix It)

Let's be honest: your first few loaves might not turn out perfect. And that's okay.

Bread is a living, breathing craft. Even with the precision of a bread machine like the Cuisinart, things can go off course. Maybe your loaf rose too high and collapsed. Maybe it came out with a dense, gummy center. Or maybe it just didn't rise at all and you're wondering what went wrong.

This chapter exists to calm your nerves and build your baking instincts. Because once you know what went wrong, fixing it becomes easy and next time, you'll get it just right.

Let's troubleshoot the most common loaf fails, one crumb at a time.

Common Mistakes Solved

Loaf Is Too Dense or Heavy

What it looks like: Thick, brick-like texture. No airy rise.

Possible causes:

- Too much flour (especially if scooped, not spooned & leveled)
- Not enough yeast
- Old or inactive yeast
- Water was too hot and killed the yeast
- Used all-purpose flour when bread flour was needed

Fix it next time:

- Measure flour carefully using the spoon & level method

- Check yeast freshness—store in the fridge and replace every few months
- Use warm water (not hot)—around 110°F (43°C)
- Use bread flour for higher gluten strength

Loaf Rose, Then Collapsed

What it looks like: Puffy top during baking that sinks like a crater afterward

Possible causes:

- Too much yeast or sugar (causes over-rising and collapsing)
- Not enough salt (salt helps control yeast activity)
- Too much liquid
- Opened the lid during rising or baking
- Weak flour structure

Fix it next time:

- Stick closely to recipe measurements—especially yeast and sugar
- Always include salt (unless medically restricted)
- Don't open the lid once rising has begun
- Consider switching to bread flour for more support

Gummy or Undercooked Center

What it looks like: Bread looks baked outside but doughy inside

Possible causes:

- Too much liquid
- Machine's baking time too short
- Bread was removed too early
- Cold or refrigerated ingredients used
- Loaf size setting didn't match recipe

Fix it next time:

- Double-check your recipe's liquid measurement
- Allow the loaf to rest in the pan for 10–15 minutes before slicing
- Use room-temperature ingredients
- If needed, run an extra "Bake Only" cycle for 10–15 minutes

Crust Too Thick or Hard

What it looks like: Tough outer shell, almost too hard to slice

Possible causes:

- Dark crust setting selected
- Bread was left in "Keep Warm" mode for too long
- Not enough fat in dough (fat softens the crust)

Fix it next time:

- Choose a light or medium crust color
- Remove the loaf as soon as it's done
- Consider adding a tablespoon of oil or butter to soften the result

Ingredients Didn't Mix Properly

What it looks like: Flour sticking to corners, uneven texture, dry patches

Possible causes:

- Kneading paddle wasn't attached properly
- Ingredients added in wrong order
- Machine wasn't on a level surface
- Too much dry ingredient, not enough liquid

Fix it next time:

- Double-check that the kneading paddle is securely locked into place

- Add liquids first, then dry, then yeast (unless otherwise stated)
- Use a spatula early in kneading to help guide flour into the mix (just once)

Fixes & Preventative Tips

Here are some universal best practices to help avoid issues before they happen:

1. Always Measure Carefully

- Use the correct cups and spoons (dry for dry, liquid for liquid)
- Spoon and level flour—don't scoop directly from the bag
- Don't eyeball yeast or salt; a little too much goes a long way

2. Check the Yeast

- Old yeast is one of the top reasons loaves fail

- Keep it sealed in a cool, dry place (preferably refrigerated)
- If in doubt, proof it: mix a small amount with warm water and sugar to test activity

3. Use Room Temperature Ingredients

- Cold eggs, milk, or water can slow yeast activity
- Let ingredients sit on the counter for 20 minutes before starting

4. Stick to the Right Order

- For Cuisinart machines, the general order is:

1. Liquids (water, oil, eggs)
2. Sweeteners
3. Salt
4. Flour
5. Yeast (on top)

5. Leave It Alone During Rise and Bake

- Avoid opening the lid once the dough has started rising
- A sudden loss of heat can ruin your loaf's structure

6. Clean Your Machine Regularly

- Leftover flour or sticky dough can interfere with paddles and cycles
- Wait until the machine is fully cool, then wipe it out with a damp cloth

Final Encouragement: One "Bad" Loaf Is Not a Failure

Even professional bakers have loaves that flop. What matters most is what you learn from each one. If your bread comes out wrong, don't toss the machine or lose confidence. Ask yourself what may have gone wrong, refer back to this chapter, and try again. Odds are, the next loaf will be dramatically better.

And once you land your first golden-crusted, perfectly risen, airy, warm-from-the-pan masterpiece?

You'll know it was all worth it.

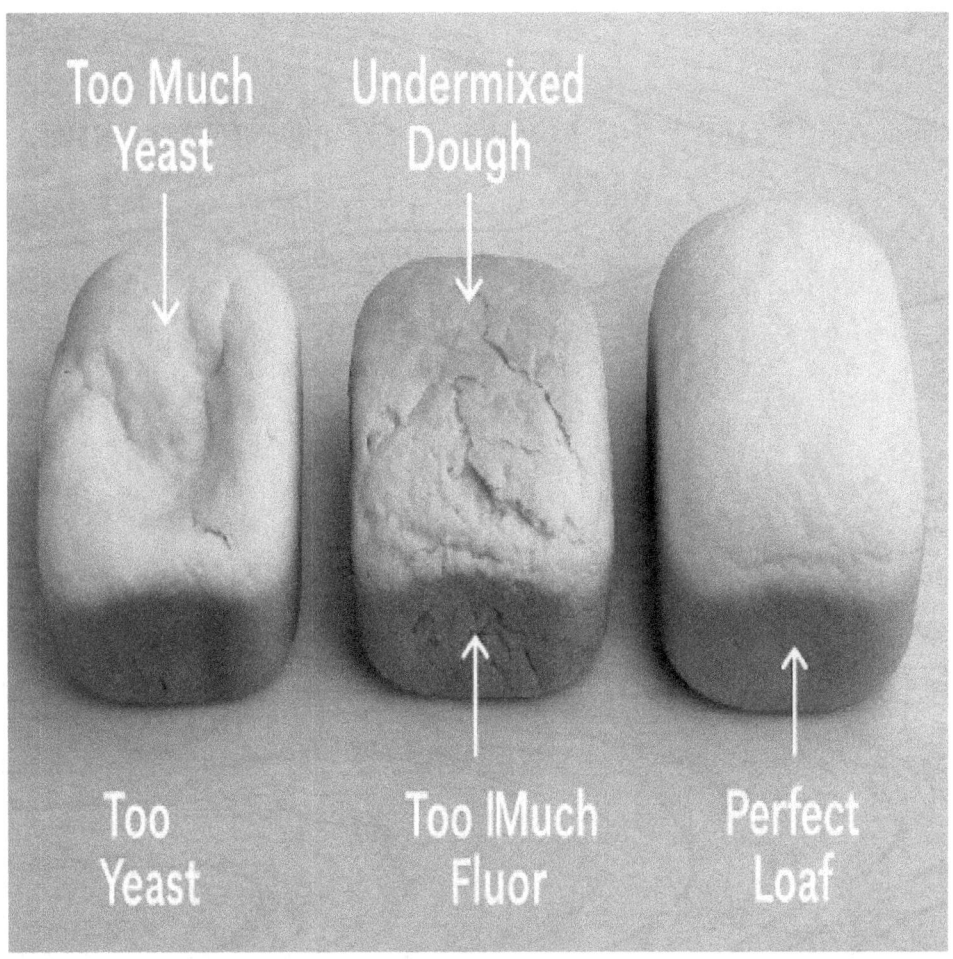

PART 2: 101 FOOLPROOF CUISINART BREAD RECIPES

Chapter 4

White Breads – Soft, Fluffy, Versatile

White bread may be the simplest of breads but don't mistake it for basic. When done right, it's everything: pillowy inside, golden outside, rich with the aroma of warm flour and just enough sweetness to toast like a dream. It's the sandwich base you crave, the soup sidekick you love, and the everyday hero that brings smiles to the breakfast table.

These 20 recipes are designed to show you what's possible with white bread: from farmhouse loaves to cheesy herb creations, garlic-kissed slices to yogurt-softened buns. And every single one starts with the press of a button.

How These Recipes Work

Each recipe in this chapter includes:

- Simple ingredient lists (no more than 10 items)
- Fast prep (usually under 10 minutes)
- Loaf size recommendations (default is 1.5 lb unless noted)
- Crust suggestions (light, medium, or dark)
- "Make-It-Yours" tips for swaps or flavor twists

All recipes follow the standard order of ingredients unless otherwise noted:

1. Liquids
2. Sweeteners & fats
3. Salt
4. Flour
5. Yeast
6. Let's bake.

1. Classic White Sandwich Bread

The gold standard. Soft, sliceable, and perfect for

sandwiches or toast.

- Water
- Butter
- Sugar
- Salt
- Bread flour
- Instant yeast

Make-It-Yours: Add 2 tbsp dry milk powder for added softness.

2. Farmhouse Buttermilk Loaf

Tangy, soft, and great with jam.

- Buttermilk
- Butter
- Sugar
- Salt
- Bread flour

- Instant yeast

Make-It-Yours: Add 1 tsp dill or rosemary for a savory twist.

3. Country White Honey Bread

Gentle sweetness with a golden crust.

- Water
- Honey
- Butter
- Salt
- Bread flour
- Instant yeast

Make-It-Yours: Use maple syrup instead of honey.

4. Crusty French White Bread

Chewy crust with a soft, airy crumb.

- Water
- Olive oil
- Salt
- Bread flour
- Instant yeast

Make-It-Yours: Let rest 10 minutes after cycle ends before slicing for a crispier shell.

5. Milk & Butter White Bread

Extra rich and soft, ideal for kids.

- Whole milk
- Butter
- Sugar
- Salt
- Bread flour
- Instant yeast

Make-It-Yours: Add 1 egg for added richness and color.

6. Olive Oil Country Loaf

Slightly savory and soft with a golden crust.

- Water
- Olive oil
- Salt
- Bread flour
- Instant yeast

Make-It-Yours: Add crushed garlic or rosemary before the knead beep.

7. Garlic Herb White Bread

The ultimate sandwich upgrade.

- Water
- Butter

- Sugar
- Garlic powder
- Italian seasoning
- Salt
- Bread flour
- Instant yeast

Make-It-Yours: Add ½ cup shredded mozzarella during add-in beep.

8. Mozzarella Basil White Bread

Soft, cheesy, and perfect for tomato soup.

- Water
- Olive oil
- Sugar
- Salt
- Bread flour
- Shredded mozzarella

- Dried basil
- Instant yeast

Make-It-Yours: Substitute cheddar or gouda for a different flavor note.

9. Onion Dill Bread

A savory loaf with flavor in every bite.

- Water
- Butter
- Sugar
- Dried onion flakes
- Dried dill
- Salt
- Bread flour
- Instant yeast

Make-It-Yours: Add 1 tbsp Greek yogurt for extra

moisture.

10. Sesame White Loaf

Toasty crust, nutty finish.

- Water
- Butter
- Sugar
- Salt
- Bread flour
- Sesame seeds
- Instant yeast

Make-It-Yours: Brush loaf with egg wash and sprinkle extra seeds before final rise.

11. Parmesan Herb Bread

Savory, cheesy, perfect for slicing thick and toasting.

- Water
- Olive oil
- Grated parmesan
- Garlic powder
- Italian herbs
- Salt
- Bread flour
- Instant yeast

Make-It-Yours: Add a pinch of red pepper flakes for heat.

12. Yogurt & Honey White Bread

Subtly sweet, pillowy soft, with a tender chew.

- Greek yogurt
- Honey
- Olive oil
- Salt
- Bread flour

- Instant yeast

Make-It-Yours: Add a pinch of cinnamon and raisins for a sweet breakfast loaf.

13. Potato White Bread

Extra moist and slightly sweet.

- Mashed potatoes
- Water
- Butter
- Sugar
- Salt
- Bread flour
- Instant yeast

Make-It-Yours: Add chopped chives or rosemary.

14. Southern Cornmeal White Bread

White bread with a cornbread heart.

- Water
- Butter
- Sugar
- Salt
- Bread flour
- Cornmeal
- Instant yeast

Make-It-Yours: Add shredded cheddar during add-in cycle.

15. White Dinner Rolls (Pan Baked)

Use dough cycle to shape and bake in muffin tins or a baking sheet.

- Milk
- Butter
- Sugar
- Salt
- Bread flour
- Instant yeast

Make-It-Yours: Brush with melted butter and sprinkle sea salt before baking.

16. Cheddar White Bread

Cheese lovers' dream.

- Water
- Butter
- Sugar
- Salt
- Bread flour
- Shredded cheddar

- Instant yeast

Make-It-Yours: Add bacon bits or green onions during knead beep.

17. Greek Yogurt White Bread

High-protein softness with a light tang.

- Greek yogurt
- Water
- Olive oil
- Sugar
- Salt
- Bread flour
- Instant yeast

Make-It-Yours: Add cracked pepper and herbs.

18. Rustic Italian Loaf

Simple, chewy, made for bruschetta.

- Water
- Olive oil
- Salt
- Bread flour
- Instant yeast

Make-It-Yours: Add chopped sun-dried tomatoes or olives.

19. Soft Pull-Apart Bread (Use Dough Cycle)

Perfect for shareable rolls or monkey bread.

- Water
- Butter

- Sugar
- Salt
- Bread flour
- Instant yeast

Make-It-Yours: Roll in cinnamon sugar before shaping and baking.

20. Beginner's Everyday White Bread

When in doubt, make this loaf.

- Water
- Butter
- Sugar
- Salt
- Bread flour
- Instant yeast

Make-It-Yours: Use milk instead of water for a softer crumb.

With white bread, simplicity becomes comfort—and this chapter gives you the foundation for so much more to come. As you move into wheat, sweet, and gluten-free breads, remember: every great baker starts here.

Chapter 5

Whole Wheat & Multigrain Breads – Nutritious and Fiber-Rich

Whole wheat bread doesn't just nourish your body—it fills your kitchen with the warm, earthy aroma of care. Multigrain breads add layers of texture and depth, making every bite satisfying and substantial.

In this chapter, we go beyond "just healthy" and bring you loaves that feel **wholesome**, not heavy. Each one is designed for flavor, nutrition, and the kind of crust that crunches just enough to let you know it's real.

Whether you're adding fiber to your day, fueling your mornings, or building a better sandwich, these 20 recipes will become pantry staples.

Recipe Notes

- Most loaves are **1.5 lb size**, adjustable to 1 or 2 lb as needed.
- All use **bread machine whole wheat or whole grain settings** (usually Menu 3).
- For best results, use **white whole wheat flour or bread flour blend** for lighter texture.
- Follow the order: **liquids first, yeast last**.

1. 100% Whole Wheat Sandwich Bread

Classic, hearty, and slightly sweet.

Make-It-Yours: Add 1 tbsp molasses or maple syrup for depth.

2. Honey Wheat Bread

A bakery favorite. Tender, slightly sweet, and perfect for sandwiches.

Make-It-Yours: Sprinkle sesame seeds on top before baking.

3. Oatmeal Wheat Loaf

Soft crumb, nutty texture, and extra fiber.

Make-It-Yours: Add 1 tsp cinnamon + ¼ cup raisins for a breakfast version.

4. Flaxseed & Wheat Fiber Bread

Loaded with omega-3s and great for digestion.

Make-It-Yours: Add chia or sunflower seeds for a protein boost.

5. Multigrain Seed Bread

A powerhouse loaf packed with crunch.

Make-It-Yours: Add 2 tbsp pepitas or hemp seeds for extra texture.

6. Cinnamon Raisin Wheat Bread

Perfectly sweet and hearty—great for toasting.

Make-It-Yours: Use golden raisins and a swirl of brown sugar for variety.

7. Sunflower Seed Whole Wheat

Crunchy, rich, and earthy.

Make-It-Yours: Top with rolled oats before baking.

8. Molasses Wheat Loaf

Deeply flavorful with a soft, almost cake-like crumb.

Make-It-Yours: Add ¼ tsp ground ginger for warmth.

9. Cracked Wheat Rustic Bread

Chunky and rustic—ideal for hearty soups.

Make-It-Yours: Stir in caramelized onions or roasted garlic during add-in beep.

10. Barley & Wheat Country Bread

Slightly chewy, old-world texture with real body.

Make-It-Yours: Add shredded sharp cheddar for savory flavor.

11. Rye-Infused Wheat Bread

Balanced flavor, not too sour. Light enough for sandwiches.

Make-It-Yours: Add caraway seeds for traditional rye notes.

12. Chia & Quinoa Wheat Loaf

Protein-packed and full of modern nutrition.

Make-It-Yours: Add chopped walnuts for crunch.

13. Whole Wheat English Muffin Bread

Crusty, tangy, and perfect for slicing and toasting.

Make-It-Yours: Dust the pan with cornmeal before baking.

14. Harvest Grain Bread

Inspired by bakery grain loaves—full of seeds and flavor.

Make-It-Yours: Add dried cranberries and flax for a trail-mix twist.

15. Spelt & Wheat Loaf

Gentle nutty flavor, mild on the stomach.

Make-It-Yours: Use part almond flour for softness and added richness.

16. Millet Multigrain Bread

Tiny pearls of crunch with a mild base.

Make-It-Yours: Add thyme and lemon zest for an herby twist.

17. Ancient Grains Power Bread

Amaranth, teff, buckwheat—bread with history and heart.

Make-It-Yours: Use coconut oil for subtle sweetness.

18. Apple Walnut Wheat Bread

Chunky, chewy, and subtly sweet.

Make-It-Yours: Add shredded carrots or dried cranberries.

19. Brown Rice & Wheat Bread

Great gluten-alternative loaf that's still soft and sturdy.

Make-It-Yours: Add roasted sesame oil for an Asian-inspired flavor.

20. Hearty Breakfast Wheat Loaf

Wheat + oats + fruit = the ultimate morning loaf.

Make-It-Yours: Add ½ tsp vanilla extract and a dash of nutmeg.

Each of these loaves is made with purpose and nourishment in mind. They're meant to be enjoyed slowly—with butter and honey, avocado and eggs, or toasted with jam. Bread can be healthy and delicious—and your Cuisinart makes it easier than ever to have both.

Chapter 6

Sweet Breads & Treat Loaves – Perfect for Breakfast or Dessert

Sweet breads in a Cuisinart bread machine are a revelation. They deliver all the indulgence of a bakery loaf with none of the fuss. Whether you're craving a cinnamon swirl for breakfast, a banana loaf for snacking, or a chocolate-studded brioche to impress your guests—these recipes rise to the occasion.

Each one is:

- **Soft and fragrant**
- **Perfectly balanced in sweetness**
- **Baked start-to-finish in your bread machine**, unless noted otherwise for dough-shaping loaves

All recipes use the **"Sweet"** or **"Basic"** cycle depending on ingredients and texture.

1. Classic Cinnamon Swirl Bread

A breakfast classic with ribbons of sugar and spice.

Make-It-Yours: Add chopped pecans or raisins to the swirl.

2. Chocolate Chip Brioche

Rich, buttery, and filled with semi-sweet chips.

Make-It-Yours: Swap chocolate chips for white chocolate and dried cranberries.

3. Banana Nut Bread

Moist, fragrant, and loaded with ripe banana flavor.

Make-It-Yours: Add a dash of nutmeg or ½ tsp espresso powder.

4. Apple Cinnamon Bread

Chunks of fresh apple in a spiced, tender loaf.

Make-It-Yours: Use applesauce in place of some water for deeper flavor.

5. Sweet Vanilla Milk Bread

Soft, lightly sweet, and perfect with jam or butter.

Make-It-Yours: Add a few drops of almond extract for a bakery-style twist.

6. Pumpkin Spice Loaf

Autumn in a loaf pan—rich, spiced, and soft.

Make-It-Yours: Add mini chocolate chips or top with pepitas.

7. Blueberry Lemon Bread

Zesty and fresh with bursts of blueberry sweetness.

Make-It-Yours: Try with raspberries or blackberries.

8. Maple Pecan Breakfast Bread

Sweetened with real maple syrup and topped with crunchy nuts.

Make-It-Yours: Add a cinnamon glaze after baking.

9. Almond Coconut Bread

Tropical sweetness in a light, moist loaf.

Make-It-Yours: Sprinkle shredded coconut on top during last rise.

10. Raisin Date Loaf

A darker, fruitier bread with natural sweetness.

Make-It-Yours: Use chopped figs or prunes as an alternative.

11. Honey Butter Bread

Rich, smooth, and ideal with a cup of tea.

Make-It-Yours: Serve warm with salted whipped butter.

12. Mocha Chocolate Bread

Chocolate loaf with a hint of coffee in the background.

Make-It-Yours: Add chocolate chunks instead of chips for richness.

13. Strawberry Cream Cheese

Bread

Swirled with fruit and creamy filling.

Make-It-Yours: Use blueberry or raspberry preserves instead.

14. Carrot Cake Bread

All the spice and sweetness of carrot cake in sliceable form.

Make-It-Yours: Add chopped walnuts and a glaze after baking.

15. Pineapple Coconut Bread

Tropical, moist, and slightly chewy.

Make-It-Yours: Add macadamia nuts for crunch.

16. Gingerbread Loaf

Dark, spiced, and festive.

Make-It-Yours: Add orange zest or chopped crystalized ginger.

17. Cherry Almond Sweet Bread

Elegant and nutty with fruity depth.

Make-It-Yours: Top with sliced almonds and a drizzle of icing.

18. Orange Cranberry Loaf

Bright, tart, and balanced.

Make-It-Yours: Add a citrus glaze or orange peel garnish.

19. Marshmallow Chocolate Swirl

Bread

A dessert loaf that tastes like s'mores.

Make-It-Yours: Add crushed graham crackers to the swirl.

20. Birthday Cake Bread

Vanilla loaf with rainbow sprinkles and white chocolate chips.

Make-It-Yours: Drizzle with icing and add extra sprinkles on top.

These sweet breads are celebrations in a loaf pan and with your Cuisinart machine, they're simpler than ever. Whether you're prepping a breakfast treat, a lunchbox surprise, or an after-dinner slice, this chapter has something indulgent, familiar, and unforgettable.

Chapter 7

Gluten-Free Breads – Soft, Satisfying, and Wheat-Free

For many home bakers, gluten-free bread is intimidating. It doesn't behave like traditional wheat dough. It's wetter, denser, and often relies on blends of flours to create the structure gluten would typically provide.

But your **Cuisinart bread machine's gluten-free setting** changes everything. These recipes are designed to work with that setting, so the rise, knead, and bake cycles are tuned specifically for these ingredients.

Whether you're gluten-sensitive, Celiac, or just experimenting with alternatives, these loaves will surprise you. You'll get tender interiors, golden crusts, and a newfound appreciation for what gluten-free can taste like.

Tips for Gluten-Free Bread Success

- Always use **certified gluten-free flours** if baking for someone with Celiac disease.
- Most recipes will be **thicker batter-like doughs**, not traditional dry dough.
- Use **a rubber spatula** to help evenly spread the dough in the pan before baking.
- Let loaves **cool fully before slicing**—they firm up as they rest.
- Store in the fridge or slice and freeze—GF bread doesn't last long on the counter.

15 Gluten-Free Bread Machine Recipes

1. Classic Gluten-Free White Bread

Soft, sandwich-friendly, and totally dependable.

Make-It-Yours: Add a splash of apple cider vinegar for improved rise.

2. Gluten-Free Multigrain Sandwich Bread

A heartier, fiber-filled version of the classic.

Make-It-Yours: Add chia, flax, or sunflower seeds for crunch.

3. Brown Rice & Quinoa Bread

Moist and wholesome, with a nutty backbone.

Make-It-Yours: Stir in pumpkin seeds or chopped herbs.

4. Oat Flour Bread (GF Certified

Oats)

Comforting and soft with a slightly sweet flavor.

Make-It-Yours: Add cinnamon and raisins for a breakfast version.

5. Almond Flour Banana Bread

Naturally sweet and high in protein.

Make-It-Yours: Add chopped walnuts or dark chocolate chips.

6. Gluten-Free Cinnamon Raisin Bread

Soft, fragrant, and perfect for toasting.

Make-It-Yours: Swirl in a brown sugar cinnamon layer.

7. Soft Gluten-Free Dinner Rolls (use dough cycle)

Delicate texture, perfect for holiday tables.

Make-It-Yours: Brush with garlic butter or honey glaze.

8. Buckwheat Honey Bread

Rich, earthy, and great with butter and jam.

Make-It-Yours: Add dried cherries or orange zest.

9. Gluten-Free Pumpkin Bread

Spiced and seasonal, yet soft and sliceable.

Make-It-Yours: Top with pecans or coconut flakes before baking.

10. Coconut Flour Sweet Bread

Low-carb and naturally gluten-free.

Make-It-Yours: Use applesauce instead of eggs for a dairy-free version.

11. Gluten-Free Sourdough-Style Bread

Tangy and chewy without any fermentation fuss.

Make-It-Yours: Add 1 tsp apple cider vinegar + a small dollop of Greek yogurt.

12. Cheesy Herb Gluten-Free Bread

Savory and versatile—great for grilled cheese.

Make-It-Yours: Use parmesan, cheddar, or dairy-free cheese.

13. Golden Cornbread Loaf (GF)

Perfect for chili nights or BBQ.

Make-It-Yours: Add green chiles or shredded cheddar.

14. Flax & Chia Gluten-Free Bread

Rich in fiber and omega-3s, but soft and sliceable.

Make-It-Yours: Add sunflower seeds and cinnamon for a hearty twist.

15. High-Protein Gluten-Free Power Bread

A post-workout loaf that holds its shape and satisfies.

Make-It-Yours: Mix in hemp hearts, whey protein isolate, or chopped almonds.

Gluten-free bread is no longer a second-rate option. With the right blend of ingredients and the consistent control of your Cuisinart machine, these loaves rival traditional breads for taste, texture, and versatility. Every recipe here was created to show that comfort and health can live on the same slice.

Chapter 8

International & Specialty Breads – Flavors of the World from Your Countertop

Bread is one of the oldest, most universal foods on earth. Nearly every culture has its version—soft or crusty, flat or fluffy, plain or spiced and now, thanks to your Cuisinart bread machine, you can bring those global staples into your home with ease.

These 11 recipes celebrate unique flours, textures, and traditions from around the world. Some are subtly sweet, others rustic and bold but all are simplified for your bread maker, so you can enjoy cultural classics with hands-off ease.

11 Global & Specialty Bread Machine Recipes

1. Japanese Milk Bread (Shokupan)

Soft, springy, and lightly sweet—famous for its pillowy texture.

Make-It-Yours: Add 1 tbsp dry milk and 1 tbsp condensed milk for an ultra-soft crumb.

2. Irish Soda Bread (Machine-Adapted)

A denser, rustic loaf made with baking soda instead of yeast.

Make-It-Yours: Add raisins and orange zest for a festive touch.

3. German Potato Bread

Moist and hearty, with mashed potatoes folded into the dough.

Make-It-Yours: Mix in caraway seeds or sautéed onions.

4. Cuban Bread (Pan Cubano)

Slightly sweet and tender with a crisp, thin crust—perfect for sandwiches.

Make-It-Yours: Brush top with sugar water before baking for shine.

5. Moroccan Olive Bread (Khobz Zaitoun)

Fragrant with herbs and studded with black olives.

Make-It-Yours: Add preserved lemon or harissa paste for deeper spice.

6. Swedish Cardamom Bread (Kardemummabröd)

A soft, lightly sweet loaf with aromatic cardamom.

Make-It-Yours: Add pearl sugar on top or swirl with cinnamon.

7. Indian Spiced Bread

Warm spices like cumin, coriander, and turmeric in a soft, earthy loaf.

Make-It-Yours: Add a spoonful of yogurt to tenderize and enrich the dough.

8. Turkish Pide Bread (Machine-Mixed)

Chewy and golden, usually shaped by hand—here, we use the dough cycle.

Make-It-Yours: Add nigella seeds or sesame before baking.

9. Scandinavian Rye Bread

Dense and deep in flavor, often sliced thin and served with butter or smoked fish.

Make-It-Yours: Add molasses for a darker, richer version.

10. Caribbean Coconut Bread

Soft, tropical, and subtly sweet—great with butter and jam.

Make-It-Yours: Add a dash of nutmeg and shredded coconut to the dough.

11. Mediterranean Herb Focaccia (Machine-Mixed)

Olive oil–rich dough with rosemary, thyme, and sea salt—perfect for dipping.

Make-It-Yours: Use the dough cycle, then shape and bake in the oven with olive oil drizzle.

These international breads remind us that flavor knows no borders and that your bread machine can do far more than the basics. Whether you're introducing your family to new cultures or reconnecting with your heritage through food, this chapter lets you explore the world one slice at a time.

Chapter 9

Seasonal & Holiday Loaves – Festive Bakes That Make Memories

Bread has always been part of the celebration—whether it's the golden braid of a challah, the warmth of cinnamon at Christmas, or the rich fruitiness of Easter loaves. These aren't just recipes. They're rituals. They mark time, honor family, and carry the scent of cherished memories.

In this chapter, we bring you 5 seasonal favorites, each crafted to rise beautifully in your Cuisinart machine and to stand proud at your holiday table.

Whether it's winter, spring, or a weekend gathering that needs a little magic, these loaves deliver warmth, flavor, and tradition—one slice at a time.

5 Seasonal & Holiday Bread Machine Recipes

1. Classic Challah (Dough Cycle)

Soft, slightly sweet, and stunning when braided. A Jewish staple, and a family favorite year-round.

Make-It-Yours: Add raisins or a sprinkle of sesame or poppy seeds before baking.

Note: Use the dough cycle, then braid and bake in your oven for best texture and presentation.

2. Pumpkin Spice Harvest Loaf

A fall favorite—moist, warmly spiced, and fragrant.

Make-It-Yours: Add chopped pecans, dark chocolate chips, or swirl with cream cheese.

3. Italian Panettone-Style Bread

Light, airy, and rich with dried fruits and citrus zest—this machine-friendly version captures the spirit of the original.

Make-It-Yours: Mix in candied orange peel, raisins, and a splash of rum extract.

4. Cinnamon Cranberry Christmas Bread

Sweet and tart, perfect for holiday breakfast or gifting.

Make-It-Yours: Top with glaze or coarse sugar once cooled.

5. Easter Lemon Poppy Seed Loaf

Bright, buttery, and refreshing. A spring favorite with tea

or brunch.

Make-It-Yours: Drizzle with a lemon glaze or fold in cream cheese chunks before baking.

Whether you're baking to celebrate a tradition or to create a new one, these loaves carry more than just ingredients—they carry sentiment. Serve them warm, gift them with a ribbon, or bake them just for you. That's the beauty of holiday bread: it nourishes both body and memory.

Chapter 10

Beyond the Loaf – Doughs & Rolls (5 Recipes)

Your Cuisinart bread machine isn't limited to loaves. In fact, some of its greatest magic happens in the dough cycle—where it kneads and rises your dough to perfection, leaving you to shape, season, and bake as you please. This chapter is your invitation to explore that side of bread-making.

From soft dinner rolls to chewy pretzels, from herby knots to crisp pizza bases, these recipes will have you rethinking what your bread maker can do.

5 Dough & Roll Recipes for Your Bread Machine

1. Classic Dinner Rolls

Soft, pillowy, and golden brown—perfect for weeknight dinners or holiday feasts.

Make-It-Yours: Brush with garlic butter or sprinkle with sesame seeds before baking.

2. Garlic Herb Knots

Buttery knots infused with garlic, parsley, and oregano.

Make-It-Yours: Swap herbs for rosemary and thyme for a more earthy flavor.

3. New York–Style Pizza Dough

Thin, crisp edges with a chewy center—restaurant quality

from home.

Make-It-Yours: Add 1 tbsp olive oil and a pinch of sugar for a softer crust.

4. Soft Pretzels

Golden, chewy, and sprinkled with coarse salt—perfect for game day.

Make-It-Yours: Try cinnamon sugar instead of salt for a sweet twist.

5. Cinnamon Swirl Rolls

Soft spirals filled with cinnamon sugar and drizzled with icing.

Make-It-Yours: Add chopped pecans or swap cinnamon for cocoa powder.

Pro Tip: *When using the dough cycle, let the machine do all the kneading and rising, but finish the baking in your oven for the best texture and presentation.*

This chapter reminds you: the bread machine is just the beginning—your creativity takes it the rest of the way.

Chapter 11

7-Day Beginner Bread Bootcamp

Starting with your bread machine can feel like standing in front of a piano for the first time—full of potential but a little intimidating. That's why this bootcamp is here: to walk you through seven consecutive days of baking, each day building on the last. By the end, you'll be turning out bakery-worthy loaves with ease.

The 7-Day Plan

Day 1 – Simple White Sandwich Bread

Your warm-up loaf: light, fluffy, and perfect for any meal.

Goal: Learn ingredient order and basic cycle.

Day 2 – Honey Wheat Bread

A gentle introduction to whole grains with a touch of sweetness.

Goal: Practice with mixed flours.

Day 3 – Cinnamon Raisin Breakfast Bread

Fragrant and sweet, ideal for morning toast.

Goal: Add mix-ins without disrupting the dough.

Day 4 – Rustic French Loaf

Chewy crust, airy interior—perfect for dipping in soups.

Goal: Adjust crust settings and cycle times.

Day 5 – Multigrain Energy Bread

Packed with seeds and grains for hearty sandwiches.

Goal: Learn even seed distribution.

Day 6 – Gluten-Free Sandwich Bread

Soft, moist, and wheat-free.

Goal: Work with non-gluten flours.

Day 7 – Celebration Sweet Bread

A lightly sweet, festive loaf to end your week.

Goal: Combine skills—perfect rise, balanced sweetness, beautiful finish.

Bootcamp Tips:

- Keep notes each day on texture, taste, and adjustments.
- Use the same measuring method daily for consistency.
- Don't skip cooling time—flavors settle as bread rests.

By Day 7, you'll have gone from "unsure beginner" to "confident bread maker," with a repertoire of recipes you can bake for life.

PART 3: BREAD LOVER'S TOOLKIT

Chapter 12

Storing, Slicing & Serving Your Bread

Baking the perfect loaf is only half the story. How you store, slice, and serve your bread can mean the difference between enjoying a bakery-fresh bite or ending up with a stale, crumbly disappointment. In this chapter, you'll learn how to keep your bread tasting as good as the moment it left your machine.

Best Storage Techniques

- **Short-Term (1–2 days):** Store at room temperature in a linen bread bag or wrapped loosely in parchment paper to keep the crust from going soft. Avoid plastic unless you prefer a softer crust.
- **Medium-Term (up to 1 week):** Use a wooden bread box to allow airflow while preventing drying.

- **Long-Term (up to 3 months):** Slice the bread, wrap tightly in freezer-safe bags, and freeze. Thaw at room temperature or warm gently in the oven.

Pro Tip: *Never refrigerate bread—it accelerates staling.*

Proper Slicing Tools

- **Serrated Bread Knife:** The best way to cut without squashing your loaf.
- **Bread Slicing Guide:** Keeps slices even and sandwich-ready.
- **Cutting Board with Crumb Catcher:** Keeps your counter clean and crumb-free.

Serving Suggestions

- **Everyday Sandwiches:** Soft white or honey wheat bread for fresh lunches.

- **Toast & Spreads:** Whole wheat with almond butter, or sweet breads with jam.
- **Dinner Accompaniments:** Serve multigrain bread with soups, or crusty loaves with olive oil and balsamic vinegar.
- **Festive Occasions:** Shape rolls or braids for holiday tables.

Final Tip: Treat your bread like fresh produce—it has a short natural life, so store it thoughtfully and enjoy it at its peak.

Chapter 13

Make It Your Way – Customizing Recipes

Your bread machine recipes aren't just formulas—they're starting points. Once you understand the basics, you can tweak flavors, textures, and nutrition to suit your preferences or dietary needs. In this chapter, you'll learn how to master the art of customization without compromising loaf quality.

Add-Ins & Flavors

- **Seeds & Nuts:** Sunflower seeds, pumpkin seeds, walnuts — add during the "Add-In" beep to prevent crushing.
- **Dried Fruits:** Raisins, cranberries, chopped apricots — toss in a bit of flour before adding to prevent sinking.

- **Herbs & Spices:** Rosemary, thyme, cinnamon, cardamom — blend into the flour for even distribution.
- **Savory Extras:** Shredded cheese, roasted garlic, caramelized onions — mix late in the kneading cycle.

Dietary Modifications

- **Vegan:** Replace butter with coconut oil or olive oil; swap milk with almond, oat, or soy milk.
- **Dairy-Free:** Use plant-based butters or oils; opt for dairy-free cheese for savory breads.
- **Egg-Free:** Use flax eggs (1 tbsp flaxseed meal + 3 tbsp water) for binding in enriched breads.

Boosting Nutrition

- **High-Protein:** Add protein powder (reduce flour slightly), Greek yogurt, or quinoa flour.
- **Fiber-Rich:** Substitute part of the flour with oat bran, flaxseed meal, or chia seeds.
- **Low-Sodium:** Reduce salt and boost flavor with herbs, garlic, or nutritional yeast.

***Pro Tip:** When experimenting, change only one element at a time so you can see exactly how it affects the outcome.*

Chapter 14

Ingredient Conversion Guide

Successful bread making depends on precision. While many recipes in this book use cups and spoons, measuring by weight ensures consistent results — especially if you bake often or customize recipes.

FLOUR

- **All-Purpose Flour**

1 cup = 120 g = 4.25 oz

- **Whole Wheat Flour**

1 cup = 130 g = 4.6 oz

- **Bread Flour**

1 cup = 125 g = 4.4 oz

- **Gluten-Free Flour Blend**

1 cup = 140 g = 5 oz

SUGARS & SWEETENERS

- **Granulated Sugar**

1 cup = 200 g = 7 oz

- **Brown Sugar (Packed)**

1 cup = 220 g = 7.75 oz

- **Honey**

1 cup = 340 g = 12 oz

FATS

- **Butter**

1 cup = 227 g = 8 oz

- **Oil (Vegetable, Olive, etc.)**

1 cup = 220 g = 7.75 oz

LIQUIDS

- **Water/Milk**

1 cup = 240 ml = 8 fl oz

YEAST

- **Active Dry Yeast**

1 tbsp = 9 g = 0.32 oz

- **Instant Yeast**

1 tbsp = 10 g = 0.35 oz

QUICK CONVERSION TABLE

Cups/Spoons	Grams (g)	Ounces (oz)
1 cup flour	120–140 g	4.25–5 oz
1 cup sugar	200–220 g	7–7.75 oz
1 tbsp yeast	9–10 g	0.32–0.35 oz

Pro Tip:

Scoop flour into your cup with a spoon, then level it off.

Avoid dipping the cup directly into the flour bag, as this can pack it down and throw off measurements.

Chapter 15

Bread Machine Glossary

Whether you're brand new to bread making or just need a refresher, these terms will help you feel at home with your Cuisinart bread machine.

Add-Ins

Extra ingredients such as nuts, seeds, herbs, dried fruit, or chocolate chips added during the bread-making cycle. Often added at the "beep" or during the mix phase to avoid being overmixed or crushed.

Crumb

The interior texture of the bread. Fine and even crumb is great for sandwich loaves, while an open, airy crumb is typical of rustic artisan bread.

Cycle

The programmed stages your bread machine runs through — kneading, rising, and baking — depending on the selected setting.

Dough Cycle

A setting that prepares dough for shaping and baking in a conventional oven, rather than completing the baking in the bread machine.

Gluten Development

The process of forming strong gluten strands in the dough, giving bread its structure and chewiness.

Kneading Paddle

The removable metal or non-stick blade inside the bread pan that mixes and kneads your dough.

Proofing

The final rise before baking, allowing the dough to expand and develop flavor.

Rise Time

The period during which the dough rests and expands due to yeast activity. Often repeated in multiple stages in certain recipes.

Starter

A fermented mixture of flour and water used to develop natural yeast and bacteria for baking sourdough or specialty breads.

Windowpane Test

A quick way to check gluten development: stretch a small piece of dough between your fingers. If it forms a thin, translucent "window" without tearing, the gluten is well-developed.

Pro Tip: Bookmark this glossary! Many of these terms will pop up in recipes throughout the book — knowing them will help you bake like a pro.

Acknowledgments

To the quiet hum of my bread machine and the scent of warm loaves that filled my kitchen—I'm grateful for every imperfect batch that led to something better.

To the home bakers who inspired this project with their questions, flops, and triumphs—this book is for you.

And to my family, whose patience, taste-testing, and honest feedback brought every recipe to life—thank you for reminding me that the best things are shared fresh, warm, and made with love.